The Cybersecurity to English Dictionary

D1262633

Raef Meeuwisse

Cyber Simplicity Ltd, Hythe, KENT, UK.   CT21 5HE.

Email:	orders@cybersimplicity.com
Twitter:	@grcarchitect
First Printing:	February 2016
Second Edition:	June 2016
Edition Date:	12 June 2016
Published by:	Cyber Simplicity Ltd

www.cybersimplicity.com

www.cybersecuritytoenglish.com

Ordering Information:

Special discounts are available on quantity purchases by corporations, associations, educators, and others. For details, contact the publisher at the above listed address.

Trade and wholesalers: Please contact Cyber Simplicity Ltd.

Tel/Fax: +44(0)1227 540 540

ISBN-13:   978-1-911452-05-8

DEDICATION

My thanks to all the readers of 'Cybersecurity for Beginners' for their ongoing feedback and additional suggestions for cybersecurity related terms. Keep them coming via Twitter: #cybersecurityforbeginners @grcarchitect

Risk does not respect bureaucracy.

Also Available

Also available from this author in paperback & digital formats:

Cybersecurity for Beginners

This book provides an easy insight into the full discipline of cybersecurity, even if you have a non-technical background.

Cybersecurity: Home and Small Business

This book is designed to provide guidance on the basic security practices we can apply at home or in small businesses to help decrease the risk of being successfully attacked. The guidance is kept simple, short and easy to follow, even if you have no technical knowledge.

The Encrypted Book of Passwords

Writing your passwords down is usually fraught with risks. The encrypted book of passwords helps you to store your passwords more securely in a format that you can read but others will find hard to break.

Pocketbook, paperback and hardback version only for this title.

Visit www.cybersimplicity.com for a full list of the latest titles.

Looking for great corporate promotional gifts?
Check out our offers at www.cybersimplicity.com

Raef Meeuwisse

CONTENTS

Raef Meeuwisse

INTRODUCTION

Have you ever been to one of those meetings where they throw out a new term and you need to find out what it means as soon as possible? The field of cybersecurity is stacked full of new words and phrases. Without easy access to a set of cybersecurity definitions, life can be hard.

You can be on top of all the main terms that are used by cybersecurity professionals. You may even find some words you can throw into the mix to impress your colleagues.

Finally you will be able to translate what a cybersecurity professional says into plain English:

*'We got **doxxed** and **pwned** by a **hacktivist** through a **RAT** takedown.'*

Becomes:

'We got our **personal information revealed** in a **humiliating attack** by a **rogue individual trying to prove a political point** using a **remote access tool** to create **widespread intrusion and disruption** to our organization.

This dictionary began life as a section of definitions at the back of my book *Cybersecurity for Beginners*.

As I wrote that book, it became apparent that there was no easy to read repository for understanding all of the main terms used in the field of cybersecurity. Due to space and size limitations, I could not include all the terms in that book, so I have set about creating a specific, expanded dictionary as a separate (and cheaper) publication.

My aim with this dictionary is to provide easy, fast access to straightforward definitions of the most frequently encountered terms used in the field of cybersecurity.

In this second edition of the dictionary I have added even more terms that I have come across that are useful for any general discussions about cybersecurity. You can even get to know the difference between terms like cryptanalysis, cryptology and cryptography.

As there are so many pieces of malware now in existence, I have not clogged the book with hundreds of names for known, specific malware threats, although I have included a very small number of the most infamous common vulnerabilities and exposures (CVE's).

Please note that where a term has more than one form, for example it exists as both an acronym and a short set of words, the definition has been placed against the most frequently used version. For example, the term *OWASP* is usually used to refer to the **O**pen **W**eb **A**pplication **S**ecurity **P**roject so the definition is located against the acronym because that is the most frequently used form of that term. There is still an entry for the *Open Web Application Security Project* that asks the reader to refer to the *OWASP* entry to view the definition.

If a term is more frequently used in its fuller form, the acronym will still be present but will refer the reader to the more commonly used form to view the definition.

If you have any additional terms that you would like to have defined or definitions you would like to have improved, please feel free to tweet me on **@grcarchitect** and I will aim to add the best suggestions to future versions.

If you are interested in getting to grips with the basics of cybersecurity, I recommend my other book 'Cybersecurity for Beginners'.

The Cybersecurity to English Dictionary

Second Edition

Raef Meeuwisse

THE CYBERSECURITY TO ENGLISH DICTIONARY

A is for Advanced Persistent Threats

acceptable use policy – a set of wording to define an agreement between any user and the enterprise that owns the service, **application** or **device** being accessed. The agreement would usually define both the primary permitted and prohibited activities.

access controls – the ability to manage and restrict entry or exit to a physical, virtual or digital area through the use of permissions. Permissions are usually assigned individually to a person, device or application service to ensure accountability and traceability of usage. The permissions can be secured using (i) physical tokens (something you have) for example a key card, (ii) secret information (something you know) such as a password or (iii) or biometric information – using part of the human body such as a fingerprint or eye scan to gain access (something you are). See also **multi-factor authentication**.

access rights – the set of permissions granted to a user account to define if they can enter and use specific functions within a network, application, system or hardware device. Usually these permissions are granted on the basis of **least privilege**. See also **least privilege**.

accountability – the security principle of ensuring that all critical assets and actions have clear ownership and traceability to identify who is responsible for them. See also **single point**

accountability.

Active memory – see **in-memory.**

adaptive content inspection (ACI) – See **deep content inspection**.

adaptive defense – the use of agile techniques to rapidly learn and adjust cyber protection methods to help decrease the possibilities of successful attack or to reduce the window of time between detection and incident counter-response. See also **indicators of compromise (IOC)**.

administrative access – any electronic account that has authority to allow elevated activities to be performed. An elevated activity is any that can apply significant changes to one or more **digital device**, software application or service. For example, the permission to install new software is considered an elevated privilege requiring this elevated authorization level.

administrative permission – the process of granting authority to a person so they can gain the type of elevated access known as **administrative access**. See **administrative access**.

Advanced Encryption Standard (AES) – this is a symmetrical method of ciphering information from plain characters to and from secret, encoded information. Symmetrical means that the same key that is used to cipher the information is used to decipher the information. This standard was originally introduced as a successor to the **Data Encryption Standard (DES)** and **Triple DES**. See also **encryption** and **symmetrical encryption**.

advanced persistent threats (APTs) – a term used to describe the tenacious and highly evolved set of tactics used by hackers to infiltrate **networks** through **digital devices** and then leave malicious software in place for as long as possible. The **cyber**

attack lifecycle usually involves the attacker performing research & reconnaissance, preparing the most effective attack tools, getting an initial foothold into the network or target **digital landscape**, spreading the infection and adjusting the range of attack tools in place and then exploiting the position to maximum advantage. The purpose can be to steal, corrupt, extort and/or disrupt an organization for financial gain, brand damage or other political purposes. This form of sophisticated attack becomes harder and more costly to resolve, the further into the lifecycle the attackers are and the longer it has managed to already remain in place. A goal with this threat type, is for the intruder to remain (persist) undetected for as long as possible in order to maximize on the opportunities of the intrusion – for example to steal data over a long period of time. See also **kill-chain**.

advanced threat defense (ATD) – very large organizations use a wider range of protective techniques to detect, deny, disrupt, degrade, deceive and contain any unauthorized attempts at entry into a digital landscape. For example, extending protection beyond anti-malware, encryption and firewalls to include the use of coordinated **network traffic analysis**, **payload analysis**, **network forensics**, **endpoint behavior analysis** and **endpoint forensics** to more actively identify and respond to emerging threats and attacks.

adware – any computer program (software) designed to render adverts to an end user. This type of software can be considered a form of malware if (i) the advertising was not consented to by the user, (ii) is made difficult to uninstall or remove, or (iii) provides other covert malware functions.

AES – see **Advanced Encryption Standard**.

all source intelligence – a term defined by the US **National Institute for Cybersecurity Education (NICE)** for gathering together threat intelligence and information across all appropriate internal and external sources for the purposes of gaining insights and implications into new and active potential threats.

air gap – to use some form of physical and electronic separation to ensure that activities in one area cannot impact or infect activities in another. Used in the context of cybersecurity to describe physically and digitally isolating sensitive or infected systems so they have no possibility of interacting with any other systems and networks.

alert status – an escalation flag that can be assigned to a security incident to indicate that it is unable to be managed inside allowable time limits or other acceptable tolerances that are defined.

anti-malware – is a computer program designed to look for specific files and behaviors (**signatures**) that indicate the presence or the attempted installation of malicious software. If or when detected, the program seeks to isolate the attack (quarantine or block the **malware**), remove it, if it can, and also alert appropriate people to the attempt or to their presence. This can be host-based (installed on devices that are directly used by people) or network based (installed on **gateway** devices where information is passed through).

anti-spyware – a subset of **anti-malware** software that has the specific purpose of detecting, blocking or preventing malicious software used to illicitly monitor and steal information. See also **spyware**.

anti-virus – predecessor of **anti-malware** software that was used before the nature and types of malicious software had diversified. This is a computer program designed to look for the presence or installation of specific files. If or when detected, the program seeks to isolate the attack (quarantine or block the **virus**), remove it, if it can, and also alert appropriate people to the attempt. A virus is only one form of mal-ware, so the term anti-malware is considered to be more inclusive of other forms of malicious software. However, as people are more familiar with the term 'anti-virus' this can sometimes be used to describe some types of anti-malware. See also **anti-malware** and **virus**.

application – a collection of functions and instructions in electronic format (a software program) that resides across one or more **digital device**, usually designed to create, modify, process, store, inspect and/or transmit specific types of data. For subversive applications, see **malware**.

APT – see **Advanced Persistent Threat.**

artificial intelligence – the development of knowledge and skills in computer programs (**applications**) to the extent that they are able to perform perception, recognition, translation and / or decision making activities without prior direct experience of the event. See also **singularity** and **digital sentience**.

assessments – the evaluation of a target (for example an **application**, service, supplier) against specific goals, objectives or other criteria through the collection of information about it. Usually, this is achieved through an established and repeatable process involving discussion or responding to questions. The purpose is to understand how closely the target meets the intended criteria and to identify any gaps or deficiencies. An assessment is different from an **audit** because it does not necessarily check for evidence and does not need to be carried out by an objective third party.

asset – any item (physical or digital) that has inherent value. For cybersecurity, information items that can be monetized (for example - intellectual property and sets of personal data) are regarded as high value assets due to their potential re-sale or blackmail value.

asymmetric backdoor – a covert entry and/or exit point that uses **cryptographic** keys set by a **malware** attacker so that only they can use it, even after it is discovered. See also **kleptography**.

asymmetric cryptography – a method of ciphering information using two different keys (a **key pair**). One is a public key, the other is a private key. One key is used to cipher the information from plain text into a secret format. The other key can then be used to decipher the secret format back to plain text. The keys can be used in any order as long as both keys are used. As one key is public, the use of the private key first is usually only for the purposes of attaching a **digital signature**. A single key cannot be used to cipher and decipher the same message. Also known as **public key encryption** and **public key cryptography**.

ATD – see **advanced threat defense.**

attack – the occurrence of an unauthorized intrusion.

attack and penetration test – see **penetration testing**.

attacker – an umbrella term to cover all types of people and organizations that may attempt to gain unauthorized access to a **digital device, application, system** or **network**. See also **black hat, hacker, hacktivist, cyber warrior, script kiddies,...**

attack lifecycle – see **cyber attack lifecycle.**

attack mechanism – a term to describe the method used to achieve an unauthorized intrusion.

attack method – the technique, tools or **exploit** used by an adversary to attempt to gain unauthorized access to any part of a **digital landscape.**

attack signature – a distinctive pattern of characteristics that can be identified to help understand and correct an attempt at unauthorized access or intrusion. See also **indicators of compromise (IOC)**.

attack surface – the sum of the potential exposure area that could be used to gain unauthorized entry to, or extraction of information. This will usually include perimeter network hardware (such as firewalls) and web servers (hardware that hosts internet enabled applications). See also **cyber defense points**.

attack vector – a path or means that could be used by an unauthorized party to gain access to a **digital device**, network or system.

audits – the use of one or more independent examiners (auditors) to check if a target product, service and/or location is meeting the specific control standards required. This form of inspection requires that individual controls are tested to confirm their suitability and consistent usage. The outcomes from this type of event, including any gaps discovered and corrective actions required are always provided in a final report.

augmented reality – the overlaying of a virtual digital layer of information on to a view of the real world. The digital layer can seem to interact with the real world but the impact is limited to affecting the perspective of the user that is immersed in the experience. This varies from **virtual reality** where the immersed use can only perceive a fully artificial world. see also **metaverse.**

authentication – the process of confirming if the identity and other properties of any entity (person or application) are valid.

authorization – the use of **authentication** information together with **access control** lists to verify if the entity (person or application) has permission to perform the function they are requesting.

availability – the assignment of a value to a set of information to indicate how much disruption or outage is considered acceptable to the owner. Often this is expressed or translated into a scale of time. Data with the highest possible **availability** rating would be required to be ready at all times (no downtime permitted), often through the use of a fully redundant failsafe. The value assigned to availability is used by the owner of an application or service to set the **recovery time objective**. See also **integrity** – a different but related term.

B is for Botnet

backdoor – an unofficial method to access software or a device that bypasses the normal authentication requirements.

backup – (i) the process of archiving a copy of something so that it can be restored following a disruption. (ii) having a redundant (secondary) capability to continue a process, service or application if the primary capability is disrupted.

bashdoor – alternative name for the family of security bugs also known as **shellshock.** See entry for **shellshock.**

BCP – see **Business Continuity Plan.**

behavior monitoring – a method of surveillance to check for actions or activities that may indicate rogue or undesirable intent.

BGP – see **Border Gateway Protocol,**

biometrics – the use of physical qualities and attributes as a form of identity authentication. Fingerprint scans, retina scans and facial recognition are all examples of biometric. As fast as new biometric options are created, the means to defeat them often follow. For this reason, biometrics is usually used only as a part of a **multi-factor authentication**.

bitcoin – a decentralized, virtual digital currency and payment system, based on a distributed, public ledger. The currency provides a high degree of transactional anonymity as balances and ledger entries are associated with private cryptographic keys and not with the individual or company that uses it (lose your key, lose your money). This has made it, along with other digital currencies a payment method of choice for illegal transactions, including making and receiving cyber blackmail payments. The invention of bitcoin is also associated with the invention of a sophisticated encryption based authenticity technique known as **blockchain**. See also **blockchain**.

black-box penetration testing – is the term used to describe a situation where no advance information about the technical details of a computer program have been made available to those who are checking it for **vulnerabilities**. They are operating without any inside knowledge, so the term is used to indicate a lack of visibility inside the 'box' (program) they are checking.

black hat – a person who engages in attempts to gain unauthorized access to one or more digital devices with nefarious (criminal or unethical) objectives. A **hacker** with unethical goals, or no perceived ethical goals.

black-listing – (in the context of cybersecurity) adding a specific file type, URL or data packet to a security defense program to prevent it from being directly accessed or used. For example, a website domain can be blocked using firewall rules to ensure that no user can visit that website through usual means.

black swan – an event that comes as a surprise, has a major impact and after analysis is falsely rationalized as predictable after the event. Some cyber **mega breaches** assert they are black swan events, however, the gaps identified during **root cause analysis** of any mega-breach always identifies at least 3 critical gaps in the standard security that would have been expected. A legitimate black swan event would not include causes that demonstrate the absence of established security countermeasures. See also **stacked risk**.

bleeding edge – using inventions so new, they have the likelihood to cause damage to their population before they become stable and safe.

blended threat – the use of a combination of a number of different **malware** techniques and/or attack methods in a single attack to increase the impact and make the intrusion harder to defeat or eliminate. See also **polymorphic malware** and **metamorphic malware** as examples.

blockchain – a method developed as part of the **cyptocurrency** known as **bitcoin** to authenticate valid transactions. A distributed, public ledger of transactions is created, with each new entry leveraging an encrypted hash value from the last entry in the ledger. This means that the ledger is stronger than previously designed authenticity techniques. Theoretical falsification of an entry would require not only the encryption to be broken or changed but also the full sequence of entries in all public copies of the ledger to be adjusted. This technique (and a private variation) is now expected to be widely adopted as a standard method for authenticity across digital platforms where authenticity is required.

blue team – the group of people that assemble during a mock attack by a **red team** to help defend the **digital landscape** being targeted.

Bluetooth – a short range wireless standard for the connection of devices.

border gateway protocol (BGP) – is a standard format that different systems on a network can use to share and make decisions on the path (routing) for information.

Bot – is a computer program designed to perform tasks. They are usually simple, small and designed to perform fast, repetitive tasks. Where the purpose of the program is in conflict with the organization, they can be considered to be a form of **malware**. See also **botnet**.

bot herder – is a **hacker** who uses automated techniques to seek vulnerable networks and systems. Their initial goal is to install or find **bot** programs they can use. Once they have one or more bots in place, they can control these to perform a larger objective of stealing, corrupting and/or disrupting information, assets and services. See also **botnet**.

bot master – alternative naming convention for a **bot herder.**

botnet – shortened version of ro**bot**ic **net**work. A connected set of programs designed to operate together over a network (including the internet) to achieve specific purposes. The purpose can be good or bad. Some programs of this type are used to help support internet connections, malicious uses include taking over control of some or all of a computers functions to support large scale service attacks (see **denial of service**). Botnets are sometimes referred to as a **zombie army**.

breach notification procedure – some types of information, when suspected or known to be lost or stolen, are required to be reported to one or more authorities within a defined time period. Usually this is when personal information is involved. The notification time period varies but is often within 24 hours. In addition to reporting the known or suspected loss to the authorities, the lead organization responsible for the information (referred to as the **data controller**) is also required to swiftly notify any people who are affected and later to submit, to appropriate regulators, a full root cause analysis and information about how they have responded and fixed any issues identified. To meet these legal obligations, larger companies usually have a pre-defined breach notification procedure to ensure that the timelines are met. The fines for data breaches are usually increased or decreased based on the adequacy of the organizations breach and **incident response** management.

brute force (attack) – the use of a systematic approach to try to gain unauthorized access. For example, if there is a single password that is only 8 characters long, there are only a finite number of possibilities that can be attempted through an automated attempt of all possible combinations. Computing speeds make brute force attempts to try millions of possibilities easy if other defenses are not present.

bug – a flaw or fault in an application or system. The term originated from very early computers that had huge capacitors that could become defective if physical insects (bugs) were present and shorted the connection.

bug bounty – a finders fee that some companies offer to people who are the first to find and report a security vulnerability in their software or service. This acts as a monetary incentive for skilled but ethical hackers to identify and report potential security gaps so the organization that owns the platform can address the issue before anyone else finds and exposes the problem.

Business Continuity Plan – (abbreviation **BCP**) an operational document that describes how an organization can restore their critical products or services to their customers should a substantial event that causes disruption to normal operations occur.

BYOC – acronym for **B**ring **Y**our **O**wn **C**loud. A term used to describe the **cybersecurity** status where employees or contractors are making direct decisions to make use of externally hosted services to manage, at least some of, their organizations work. If this is taking place without the inclusion of a process to risk assess and control the security features, it can lead to significant risks both to the direct information involved and by potentially opening up other security gaps in the **digital landscape**.

BYOD – acronym for **B**ring **Y**our **O**wn **D**evice, indicating that employees and other authorized people can bring some of their own digital devices into the work place to use for some work purposes. Some security people also use this term for 'Bring Your Own Disaster' due to the uncontrollable number of security variables that this introduces to any information allowed to flow on to or through personal devices.

C is for Cloud

CAPA – acronym meaning **c**orrective **a**ction **p**reventive **a**ction. See **corrective and preventive action system.**

CERT – acronym used widely to mean either **C**omputer **E**mergency **R**esponse **T**eam (for example CERT UK) or **C**omputer **E**mergency **R**eadiness **T**eam (for example CERT US). See also **US CERT**. The primary role of these organizations is to help their member or country organizations to prepare, monitor and respond to cybersecurity and other digital landscape threats.

certificate authority – the use of a trusted third party organization to supply and verify tokens (certificates) that attest to the validity of a technology service.

chain of custody – a method of ensuring that a set of information and any metadata (tags, labels or other descriptive additions) are preserved as they are passed between owners and locations. This term is frequently applied to the preservation of evidence in the field of **digital forensics**.

chargeware – a form of malicious software (malware) designed to perform actions on a victims device that will incur costs to them for the benefit of the attacker. For example, on a smart mobile phone, sending SMS text messages out to a premium rate number without the owners' knowledge or consent.

checksum – a method of verifying any collection of information is still exactly as it was, through the use of a mathematical algorithm. If any piece of information in the collection of information has changed, the value from running the algorithm will be changed, indicating that the information has been altered. See also **md5 hash** as an example.

Chief Information Security Officer (CISO) – a single point of accountability for ensuring that an appropriate and effective framework for managing dangers and threats is operating and effective.

cipher – the use of a key to change information into a secret or hidden format.

CISO – see **Chief Information Security Officer.**

clear box penetration testing – see **white box penetration testing.**

clickbait – to generate enticing content that encourages or pressures the recipient, or viewer, to want to access the URL link or attached file that is on offer. Originally this term was used to describe methods advertisers would use to get traffic to a particular web page, however, it is also a primary technique used to make **phishing** communications attractive to the unwary recipient.

clopen – a network or system that is intended to be run as closed and secure but due to size, scale, threats or security deficiencies is constantly identifying and seeking to eliminate new intrusions. A portmanteau of the words **clo**sed and **open**.

closed system – a collection of applications, systems and devices that only have the ability to communicate with each other. No connection to any component outside the known and trusted group is permitted.

cloud (the) – an umbrella term used to identify any technology service that uses software and equipment not physically managed or owned by the person or organization (customer) using it. This usually provides advantages of on-demand scalability at lower cost. Examples include applications that are hosted online, online file storage areas, even providing remote virtual computers. Using a cloud will mean the equipment managing the service is run by the cloud provider and not the customer. Although the customer does not own the service, they are still accountable for the information they choose to store and process through it. Usually a **cloud** service is indicated by an 'aaS' suffix. For example – **SaaS** (Software as a Service), **IaaS** (Infrastructure as a Service) and **PaaS** (Platform as a Service).

cloud security – a term used to describe the collective policies, technologies, procedures and other controls that are used to protect a technology service hosted by an external organization. Cloud platforms are typically internet accessible and shared with many customers, requiring stronger security than services delivered within an isolated network.

compartmentalization – a security technique that can be applied to high value assets. The assets can be placed in a more isolated system, network or device requiring additional security controls to access. This is designed to add greater protection to those assets.

Compliance – the process used to verify that **governance** items (policies, procedures, regulations and more) are being followed, and to identify when they are not. **Audits**, **assessments**, **continuous monitoring** can be used to identify and report deficiencies. Any identified gaps are usually tracked and resolved through a **corrective and preventive action system**.

Computer Emergency Response Team – see **CERT.**

computer virus – see **virus**

confidentiality – the assignment of a value to a set of information to indicate the level of secrecy required and used to set access restrictions. A typical example scale for confidentiality is: (i) Public Use (ii) Internal Use (iii) Confidential (iv) Strictly Confidential and (v) Restricted

configuration management – the backbone of security management in large enterprises, this is the process used to track and ensure all hardware and software are identified and in a controlled state. Functions include (i) helping to ensure that timely security **patch management** can be applied and (ii) that unknown digital devices can be prevented from connecting to the network.

consent – where electronic personal information is involved, there are often legal constraints that govern how the data can be used and where the information can be viewed, stored, transmitted or otherwise processed. In those circumstances, permission is often required from each individual for what information can be collected, where it can be processed and how long it will be retained for. These permissions can be represented by a series of tags on individual records or on the full data set. The required permission attributes can include but are not limited to, country of origin, permission for export, limitations of use, retention and notification requirements.

containment – a stage during incident response where a confirmed problem (for example a malware infection) has steps taken to isolate it and prevent the issue from spreading to other areas.

content filtering – see **packet filtering**.

continuous monitoring – using technology to actively monitor the ongoing security of an **application**, web site or other electronic service. The purpose is to provide faster alerts when any significant infringements of security that create potential risks are detected. For example, continuous automated monitoring for port scanning can detect patterns that can indicate an imminent attack and alert the appropriate personnel.

control – (in the context of security and compliance) a method of regulating something, often a process, technology or behavior, to achieve a desired outcome, usually resulting in the reduction of risk. Depending on how it is designed and used, any single control may be referred to as preventive, detective or corrective.

control information – the component of a data **packet** that provides the destination, source and type of content.

control modes – an umbrella term for preventive, detective and corrective methods of defense. Each one represents a different time posture, **preventive controls** are designed to stop an attack before it is successful, **detective controls** are designed to monitor and alert during a potential compromise and **corrective controls** are the rectification of an issue after an event.

control systems – collections of applications that function together to command the actions or activities of other devices. For example, a heating, ventilation and air-conditioning (HVAC) control system may comprise of a number of devices (sensors) that feed into a central set of applications that regulate other devices (heaters and coolers). Collectively, this would be an example of a control system. **Industrial control systems** is a term applied when the usage is for large-scale production objectives and/or to operate extremely high-capacity devices. These systems are considered high-value targets for cyber attack because they are easy to ransom, high cost to repair, have substantial ability to disrupt or halt business operations and can lead to huge brand and share-price damage.

corrective action – a specific activity (triggered by an event) that when complete will result in the mitigation or resolution of a problem. The fact the activity is triggered by an event makes the activity reactive and therefore corrective.

Corrective And Preventive Action system (CAPA) – An automated tracking process to ensure that key activities (actions) to resolve or mitigate gaps in security or compliance are consistently tracked through to completion.

corrective control – (see also control) a method of defense that is introduced as the reactive result of an observed deficiency in security. For example, the addition of greater network segmentation after an attack can be considered a corrective control

crimeware – software that has the intentional objective to perform illegal acts, such as theft or ransom. A term for a specific subset of *malware*.

critical infrastructure – the core of any digital landscape that enables the highest priority technology services and **data** flows to operate.

crack – to break into a secured **digital device**, account or service by defeating one or more security measures designed to prevent the intrusion.

cross-site scripting (also known as **XSS)** – a security exploit that takes advantage of security design flaws in web generated pages. If the dynamic pages from a legitimate site do not have very robust rules, users machines can be exploited by a 3rd party to present false links or dialog boxes that appear to be from the legitimate site but are not. A specific instance of an XSS vulnerability is known as an **XSS hole**.

cryptanalysis – the art of examining **cipher**ed information to determine how to circumvent the technique that was used to encode or hide it, i.e. analyzing ciphers.

cryptocurrency – any digital currency that makes use of **encryption** to generate and secure confidence in the units that are traded. These forms of payment are usually decentralized, unregulated and difficult to trace ownership of, making them the main form of payment for cyber crime and ransomware. See also **bitcoin** and **blockchain**.

cryptoviral extortion – the use of a specific form of **malware** that seeks to spread (install in new locations) and cipher (**encrypt**) the victims information for the purposes of demanding payment for their release. See also **ransomware**.

cryptovirus – a form of **malware** that spreads by infecting (attaching itself to) other files and makes use of cryptography, usually in the method that it attacks the victims electronic data files. The victims' files are usually ciphered (**encrypted**) so that a release fee can be demanded by the attacker. See also **ransomware**.

crytpotrojan – a form of **malware** that is designed to look initially harmless but seeks to perform an attack that involves ciphering (**encrypting**) the victims' electronic information. This technique can be used in combination with other malware and **cryptographic** techniques, usually in a **ransomware** attack. See also **blended threat**.

cryptoworm – a form of **malware** that actively seeks to spread to new locations and devices without human interaction and then makes use of cryptography, usually in the method that it attacks the victims' electronic data files. This is a sub-type of a **cryptovirus**. The technique used will actively seek to identify and make use of any available communication paths or protocols. The victims' files are usually ciphered (**encrypted**) so that a release fee can be demanded by the attacker. See also **ransomware**.

cryptographic algorithm – the use of a mathematical and/or computational model to **cipher** information from plain text to a hidden format.

cryptography – the use of models to make information secret using **ciphers** i.e. writing ciphers.

cryptology – the study of models used to make information secret using **ciphers**, i.e. reading ciphers.

crypotvirology – the study of the use of ciphers (**encryption** and **cryptography** methods), predominantly to understand how to build better cyber attacks.

CVE Identifier – the acronym stands for **C**ommon **V**ulnerabilities and **E**xposures. This is a unique number assigned in a publicly accessible database for all known (and suspected) security vulnerabilities in publicly released software. The database is maintained by the not-for-profit US MITRE Corporation. The format is CVE + Year + (number assigned) – so for example CVE-2014-6271 is the initial identifier for the shellshock security bug, with the middle number indicating it was registered in 2014. The list can be accessed through: http://cve.mitre.org/

cyber – for anything using this as a prefix, see **digital device.**

cyber attack – to take aggressive or hostile action by leveraging or targeting digital devices. The intended damage is not limited to the digital (electronic) environment.

cyber attack lifecycle – a conceptual model of the sequential steps that are involved in a successful unauthorized intrusion or disruption into a **digital landscape** or **digital device**. There are a number of models currently available, an example of the most common steps found across the models are illustrated within the definition of **advanced persistent threat**. See also **kill chain**.

cyber criminal – any person who attempts to gain unauthorized access to one or more **digital device**.

cyber defense – the collective set of technologies, processes and people that act to defend any given **digital landscape**. See also **advanced threat defense**.

cyber defense points – the digital locations where cybersecurity controls could be added. Example defense points include **data, applications, systems, devices** and **networks.**

cyber defense strategies – a short list of the primary defensive countermeasure types that can be considered at each stage in the **cyber attack lifecycle** as part of a structured defense. These are typically summarized as: detect, deny, disrupt, degrade, deceive and contain. See also **kill chain**.

cyber espionage – the use of digital technologies to help steal information from any organization or individual in order to create a financial or political gain.

cyber forensics – see **digital forensics.**

cyber threat dwell time – see **dwell time.**

cyber incident response – see **incident response.**

cyber insecurity – suffering from a concern that weaknesses in your cybersecurity are going to cause you personal or professional harm.

cyber maneuver – an action, method or process designed to operate to attack or defend all or part of **a digital landscape** in order to gain advantage over an adversary. The activity is designed to capture, disrupt, destroy, deny or otherwise manipulate the position of the adversary.

cyber operations – the activity of gathering information around active threats to the **digital landscape**. Usually a combination of real-time threat intelligence about **network** and **malware** attacks, together with external intelligence about active and emerging threats.

cyber security incident – see **security incident.**

cybersecurity – the protection of digital devices and their communication channels to keep them stable, dependable and reasonably safe from danger or threat. Usually the required protection level must be sufficient to prevent or address unauthorized access or intervention before it can lead to substantial personal, professional, organizational, financial and/or political harm. In the UK this term is used as 2 words – **cyber security**.

cybersecurity architecture – see **security architecture.**

cybersecurity control types – categories used to help organize the defenses against cyber attack. Usually these categories are (i) technical (ii) procedural (iii) physical and (iv) compliance (or legal

/ contractual). Each of the **cyber defense points** should have all of the **cyber control types** considered and in place as appropriate to the risks.

cyberspace – the area available for electronic information to exist inside any collective of interconnected **digital devices**.

cyberwar – a campaign of activities by one entity that has the purpose to defeat an enemy entity through disruption to, compromise of or theft from the enemy digital landscape. The entity can be a state, company or other organization.

cyber warrior – a person that engages in attempts at unauthorized access or disruption of digital devices, systems or networks for personal, political or religious reasons.

D is for Dwell-Time

dark internet – publicly accessible electronic data content that is only unreadable due to its format or indexing. For example, a store of raw scientific information may be internet accessible, but without indexing or context it is considered part of the dark internet. This term has a very different meaning than **dark web**.

dark net – the emergent term to describe the collection of websites that hide their server locations. Although publicly accessible, they are not registered on standard search engines and the hidden server values make it extremely difficult to locate what organizations and people are behind the site. Previously referred to mainly as the **dark web**, see also **dark internet** (different meaning in the past).

dark web – websites that hide their server locations. Although publicly accessible, they are not registered on standard search engines and the hidden server values make it extremely difficult to locate what organizations and people are behind the site.

data – information stored in an electronic or digital format

data breach notification procedure – see **breach notification procedure**.

data chain of custody – see **chain of custody.**

data controller – the organization that owns and is accountable for a set of data. In many privacy regulations around the world, the role of the data controller can have legal and financial implications for the organization and/or for a specific person (organization role) if compliance requirements are not met.

Data Encryption Standard (DES) – an early form of ciphering information from plain text to secret information using symmetrical keys, developed in around 1975. **Triple DES** is a version of the same standard that uses a bundle of keys to help increase the strength of the ciphering but still offers lower security than more recent standards. These methods are considered outdated (no longer effective) because it is now easy to break) and has been succeeded by other standards, including the **Advanced Encryption Standard**.

data loss prevention (DLP) – this term can describe both (i) technologies and (ii) the strategies used to help stop information from being taken out of an organization without the appropriate authorization. Software technologies can use heuristics (patterns that fit within certain rules), to recognize, alert and/or block data extraction activities on **digital devices**. For example, to prohibit specific types of file attachments to be sent out via internet mail services. They can also prevent or monitor many other attempts at removing or copying data. There are workarounds that can be used by skilled hackers that can evade detection by these solutions, including encryption and fragmentation. Although these solutions are becoming an essential line of defense, the most secure environments aim to prevent any significant set of data being available for export in the first place. For this reason, data loss prevention is often thought of as the last line of defense (a final safety net if all other security controls have not been successful). **Information loss prevention** (**ILP**) is an alternative version of the same term.

DDoS – acronym for **Distributed Denial of Service**. See **Denial of Service** for definition.

decapitation – (in the context of **malware**) preventing any compromised device from being able to communicate, receive instruction, send information or spread **malware** to other devices. This can effectively render many forms of malware ineffective because it removes any command, control or theft benefit. This is often a stage during **takedown** or threat removal.

deep content inspection – an advanced form of **data loss prevention** technology that allows the full set of any information being processed to be reviewed against a set of updatable rules, so that blocking, reporting, notification or other actions can be automatically applied. For example, a rule can be put in place so that if any set of 16 digit numbers (credit cards) are being sent in batches exceeding 50 from any user device, the action can be blocked and reported. Standard data loss prevention only reviews the main headers and tags, whereas this form of prevention performs a review of all the information content. Also sometimes referred to as **adaptive content inspection** (ACI) or **deep level content inspection**.

deep web – internet content that cannot be seen by search engines. This includes not only dark web content but also harmless and general content that is not indexed or generally reachable, for example - personal databases and paid content.

default accounts – generic user and password permissions, often with administrative access that is provided as standard for some applications and hardware for use during initial set-up.

defense in depth – the use of multiple layers of security techniques to help reduce the chance of a successful attack. The idea is that if one security technique fails or is bypassed, there are others that should address the attack. The latest (and correct) thinking on defense in depth is that security techniques must also consider people and operational factors (for example processes) and not just technology.

Denial of service (DoS) – an attack designed to stop or disrupt people from using organizations systems. Usually a particular section of an enterprise is targeted, for example, a specific network, system, digital device type or function. Usually these attacks originate from, and are targeted at, devices accessible through the internet. If the attack is from multiple source locations, it is referred to as a **distributed denial of service** or **DDoS** attack.

DES – acronym for **Data Encryption Standard.** See **Data Encryption Standard** for definition.

detective control – (see also **control**) a method of defense used to help identify items or issues that may occur but are not being defeated or prevented by other means. For example, an **intrusion detection system** may identify and alert a new issue but may not have the means to defeat the problem without additional intervention.

device encryption – usually refers to encoding (making unreadable) the information at rest on a smart phone, tablet, laptop or other electronic item. This encoding makes the information stored on the item readable only when a valid user is logged in.

devices – any hardware used to create, modify, process, store or transmit **data**. Computers, smart phones and USB drives are all examples of **devices**.

digital device – any electronic appliance that can create, modify, archive, retrieve or transmit information in an electronic format. Desktop computers, laptops, tablets, smart phones and internet connected home devices are all examples of **digital devices**.

digital fingerprinting – has two different potential meanings. (i) to covertly embed ownership information inside any form of electronic information, so that original ownership can still be established on stolen or copied information. This varies from **digital watermarking** because the ownership information is hidden. (ii) the use of characteristics that are unique to an electronic file or object to help prevent, detect or track unauthorized storage, usage or transmission. Used as a form of defense on high sensitivity intellectual property.

digital forensics – a specialist field to help preserve, rebuild and recover electronic information and help investigate and uncover residual evidence after an attack. See also **indicators of compromise**.

digital landscape – the collection of **digital devices** and electronic information that is visible or accessible from a particular location.

digital sentience – the development of knowledge and skills in computer programs (applications) so that they are self aware, can independently choose to acquire new skills and capabilities and express thoughts or beliefs based on observations and information acquired.

digital signature – to endorse an electronic artifact using an identity that can be verified through a mathematical technique. Digital signatures may only be considered the equivalent of their handwritten counterpart where evidence of unique access to the mathematical technique can be proven without doubt.

digital watermarking – a technique to embed ownership information inside any form of electronic information. This technique can be used towards some forms of advanced cyber defense, especially for intellectual property, so even if it is stolen, the information will still contain evidence of the original owner. See also **digital fingerprinting**.

Disaster Recovery Plan – see **Technical Disaster Recovery Plan**

Distributed Denial of Service (DDoS) – see **Denial of Service**.

DLP – see **data loss prevention.**

DNS – acronym for **d**omain **n**ame **s**ystem. Whenever a network or internet location uses a plain text name (such as www.cybersimplicity.com), this has to be translated into a specific and more technical location called the **IP address**. A service runs on a server to reconcile and translate the text value into the specific network location IP address value. This is known as a **DNS service**.

DNS service – see **DNS.**

DNS tunneling – the use of the domain name system protocol, that reconciles network locations from plain text into **IP addresses**, as a mechanism to **exfiltrate** (steal) data. **Firewalls** are used to passing DNS information to make legitimate requests across networks. By leveraging some of the values within the DNS protocol, information can potentially be transacted by an attacker hiding their data as DNS traffic.

dorking – see **Google Hacking.**

DoS – see **Denial of Service.**

doxxing (also **doxing**) – publicly exposing personal information on to the internet. Thought to be based on an abbreviation of the word 'documenting'.

drive-by download – the unintended receiving of malicious software on to a device through an internet page, electronic service or link. The victim is usually unaware that their action permitted new malicious software to be pulled on to and installed in to their digital device or network.

dual homed – any network device that has more than one network interface. The primary method of positioning **firewalls** and other network boundary or perimeter defense uses this technique to connect **untrusted networks** to **trusted networks** by keeping them isolated to different network connections and applying rules and controls on any data that is passed across.

dwell-time – in the context of cybersecurity – this refers to how long an intrusion or threat has been allowed to remain in place before being discovered and eliminated. The length of time between intrusion and detection is an indication of how successful an Advanced Persistent Threat has been. Although the dwell-time is expected to fall as cybersecurity measures mature, the average time is often hundreds of days and can be years.

dynamic host configuration protocol (DHCP) – the standard method used on networks and the internet to assign an address (internet protocol or IP) to any digital device to allow its communications to operate. This address is assigned by a server (host) each time an authorized digital device connects to it.

dynamic testing – (in the context of cybersecurity) to assess the security standards and potential **vulnerabilities** within an application or service. when it is running in an environment equivalent to the production installation. This is usually a form of **black-box penetration testing**. See also **static testing**.

E is for Exploit

encryption – the act of encoding messages so that if intercepted by an unauthorized party, they cannot be read unless the encoding mechanism can be deciphered.

endpoint – a final digital destination where electronic information is processed by users. Computers, smartphones and tablet devices are all examples of endpoints.

endpoint behavior analysis – analyzing unusual patterns on user devices, such as changes to registry entries, unusual traffic patterns or file changes as indications of potential threats or other **malware** related activity. This can contribute towards **indicators of compromise** threat intelligence.

endpoint forensics – the ability to capture both static and in-memory evidence to preserve, rebuild and uncover evidence from a known or suspected attack on a user device. See also **endpoint**.

endpoint protection – a term used to describe the collective set of security software that has become standard for most user operated **digital devices**. The security software may include anti-malware, a personal firewall, intrusion prevention and other capabilities.

ethical hacker – an alternative name for a **penetration tester.**

ethical hacking – the process of supportive (**white-hat**) **penetration test**ing experts assisting in finding security weaknesses and vulnerabilities.

event – see **security event.**

exfiltrate – to move something with a degree of secrecy sufficient not to be noticed. Used to describe moving stolen data through detection systems.

exploit – to take advantage of a security **vulnerability**. Well known exploits are often given names. Falling victim to a known exploit with a name can be a sign of low security, such as poor **patch management**.

F is for Firewall

fake website – can either be (i) a fraudulent imitation of a real internet page or site designed to look like one from the legitimate company or (ii) an internet page or site from a completely fake company, often with a 'too good to be true offer' or content. In both instances, the objectives of the site can include, to capture real log-in credentials, to receive real payments for orders that will not be delivered, to install malware.

file transfer protocol (FTP) – the standard method used to send and receive packages of information (files). **SFTP** or **secure file transfer protocol** is the secure variation of this, used to send and receive data through an encrypted connection. Even if data is sent through an encrypted connection, it will not itself be automatically encrypted.

fingerprinting – see **digital fingerprinting.**

firewall – is hardware (physical device) or software (computer program) used to monitor and protect inbound and outbound data (electronic information). It achieves this by applying a set of rules. These physical devices or computer programs are usually deployed, at a minimum, at the perimeter of each network access point. Software firewalls can also be deployed on devices to add further security. The rules applied within a firewall are known as the **firewall policy.** Advanced firewalls are often equipped with other defensive features typical for more **unified threat management**.

firewall policy – the rules applied within either a physical hardware device (a hardware firewall) or software program (a software firewall) to allow or block specific types of inbound and outbound data traffic at the perimeter of a **network** or **digital device**.

forensics – see **digital forensics.**

fuzzing – a portmanteau of **fuzz** and test**ing** to describe a method of software testing that involves entering random, unexpected, invalid and out of range data as inputs into a program. The software is then checked for any memory leaks, crashes or other flaws that result from these inputs. This can help to identify and address potential security vulnerabilities.

fuzz test – see **fuzzing.**

G is for Governance

garbage code – a technique used by some forms of **malware** to intentionally add large volumes of encrypted and irrelevant programming code to make the work of defeating the threat more difficult. The attacker can hide a very small malicious software program inside a very much larger encrypted file (potentially thousands or millions of times larger), making the process of quarantine, decryption and elimination of the threat much harder.

gateway – a point in a **network** that can be used to pass into another network. This location is a key target for cyber attacks and network level defenses.

Google dorking – alternative name for **Google hacking**. See **Google hacking.**

Google hacking – the use of search engines and other public applications and services by attackers to identify security gaps that can be exploited in a specific target. Originally, the type of easy vulnerabilities that were identified through this method led to the victims being regarded as 'dorks' or 'Google dorks'. This was because their vulnerabilities could be located through a standard search engine due to a lack of basic security configuration.

governance – the methods used by any executive to keep their organization on track with the management goals, and within acceptable performance standards. This is usually achieved by establishing **policies, procedures** and **controls** that match the enterprises vision, strategy and risk appetite.

governance, risk and compliance – a term to describe the interaction and interdependence between the activities that (i) control any organization (**governance**) (ii) verify and enforce those controls (**compliance**) and (iii) manage any substantial exposures to financial impact that emerge (**risk**), often due to gaps in (i) or (ii).

H is for Hacker

hack – the act of gaining unauthorized access to a digital device, network, system, account or other electronic data repository.

hacker – a person who engages in attempts to gain unauthorized access to one or more digital devices. Can be **black hat** (unethical) or **white hat** (**ethical hacker**) depending on the person's intent.

hacktivism – an amalgamation of hacker and activism. Describes the act of seeking unauthorized access into any digital device or digital landscape to promote a social or political agenda. Usually the unauthorized access is used to cause destruction, disruption and/or publicity. Individuals participating in these acts are called **hacktivists**.

hacktivist – an amalgamation of the words **hacker** and **activist**. Describes any individual who participates in **hacktivism**.

hashing – using a mathematical function to convert any block or group of data into a fixed length value (usually shorter than the original data) that represents the original data. This fixed length value can be used for fast indexing of large files by computer programs without the need to manage the larger data block. It is also used extensively in the field of security, for example, **digital forensics** can use this technique to verify that the data content of a copy of any examined data is identical to the original source.

Heartbleed – was the name given to the most significant security **vulnerability** (software flaw that could be taken advantage of) of its time, affecting a large number (estimated at 17%) of internet servers that used **openSSL cryptography**. It allowed vulnerable internet servers to have private encryption keys, user cookies and passwords to be stolen. A patch to fix the flaw was released on the day the vulnerability was publicly disclosed. It was given the **CVE identifier** CVE-2014-0160.

honey network – the collective name for a cluster of **honeypots** that operate together to help form part of a network intrusion detection strategy.

honeypot – an electronic device or collection of data that is designed to trap would be attackers by detecting, deflecting or otherwise counteracting their efforts. Designed to look like a real part of an enterprises attack surface, the **honeypot** will contain nothing of real value to the attacker but will contain tools to identify, isolate and trace any intrusion.

Host-based Intrusion Prevention Systems (HIPS) – a version of an **intrusion prevention system** installed directly on to the **digital device** it is protecting against exploitation. See also **intrusion prevention system** for a description of its purpose.

host-forensics – the ability to capture both static and **in-memory** evidence to preserve, rebuild and uncover evidence from a known or suspected attack on any **digital device**.

hyper text transfer protocol (HTTP) – is the standard method used to send information (files, pictures and other data) over the world wide web. **HTTPS** or **SHTTP** is the secure version of this protocol that can be used when the information requires a secure connection. It is rumored that the security for https / shttp is already or may soon be able to be broken by some organizations.

I is for Indicators Of Compromise (IOC)

IaaS – acronym meaning infrastructure as a service. This is a form of **cloud** solution where, in place of owning and running a physical network with physical servers and other hardware, the customer is offered a solution that emulates the attributes of a physical network and server infrastructure. The cloud provider operates virtualization software to offer fast, easy, infrastructure scalability at a lower cost. Ultimately, this solution still runs on physical machines maintained by the cloud provider. The cloud provider achieves the lower cost by running a much higher automation rate and utilization of the physical hardware than customers can accomplish independently.

IDAM – the collection of processes and technologies used to manage, confirm, monitor and control legitimate access to systems by authorized accounts. This includes measures to ensure each access request is from a verified, expected and legitimate person or entity.

Identity & Access Management – see **IDAM**

IDaaS – acronym for **Id**entity as a **S**ervice. The use of an authentication infrastructure that is hosted by a third party in an externally hosted solution.

IDPS – see **Intrusion Detection and Prevention System.**

ILP – see **data loss prevention.**

image steganography – to conceal information inside a picture (image file) so that the sender and/or recipient may not know that the message is present. Used within cyber attacks to help hide unauthorized or unwanted communications. For example the **Zeus** malware used an image file to communicate command and control instructions to the **malware** as **least significant bits** within a landscape image file. The recipient would perceive only an image file but the malware would be able to read the concealed message. See also **steganography** and **steganalysis**.

in-memory – any **digital device** can comprise of more than one type of **data** storage. Information that is not in active use can be stored to a device such as a hard disk. Information that is being used (or imminently expected to be used) by the processor in a computer is managed through a more active storage area (the memory or active memory). When a digital device image is captured for **digital forensic** examination, it is usual to snapshot not only the static information on any hard disk (or equivalent) but also the active information (the information in-memory).

incident – see **security incident.**

incident prediction – the use of advanced analytics to review patterns in order to foresee the most likely impending points of failure, disruption or intrusion. This can help to promote proactive enhancements in defense or enhance preparations for a specific type of incident recovery.

incident response – a prepared set of processes that should be triggered when any known or suspected event takes place that could cause material damage to an organization. The typical stages are (i) verify the event is real and identify the affected areas. (ii) contain the problem (usually by isolating, disabling or disconnecting the affected pieces). (iii) understand and eradicate the root cause. (iv) restore the affected components in their fixed state. (v) review how the process went to identify improvements to the process. An incident response may also be required to trigger other response procedures, such as a **breach notification procedure**, if there is any information which has been lost that is subject to a notification requirement. For example – the loss of any personal information beyond what might be found in a phone book entry is usually considered a notifiable event.

indicators of compromise (IOC) – is a term originally used in computer forensics to describe any observable behaviors and patterns (such as particular blocks of data, registry changes, IP address references) that strongly suggest a computer intrusion has or is taking place. The collation of these patterns and behaviors are now actively used in **advanced threat defense** to help more rapidly identify potential security issues from across a monitored digital landscape.

industrial control systems – see **control systems.**

infection – (in the context of cybersecurity) unwanted invasion by an outside agent that has intent to create damage or disruption.

information systems – see **systems.**

information loss prevention [ILP] – see **data loss prevention.**

inherent risk – the level of exposure to loss, or the impact something has before any mitigating controls are taken into consideration. For example, holding credit card data in a system brings an inherent risk to the system. See also **residual risk**.

integrity – a value that can be assigned to a set of information to indicate how sensitive it is to degradation of accuracy (such as unauthorized modification) or data loss. Loss in this context is about losing information without the ability for anyone to recover it from the system it was entered into (it is not about theft). Often this value is expressed or translated into a scale of time. For example, data with the highest possible **integrity** rating could be given a value of 'no data loss permitted'. If it was permitted to lose up to 4 hours of data that had been processed, the value would be '4 hours'. Usually if any data loss is permitted, it means that there will be other processes in place to address the loss of the electronic information. The integrity value assigned to any system or application is used to set the frequency that the information is subject to backup, or in very sensitive systems with no data loss permitted, establishes the need for a permanent secondary failover system.

Internet of Things (IoT) – the incorporation of electronics into everyday items sufficient to allow them to network (communicate) with other network capable devices. For example, to include electronics in a home thermostat so that it can be operated and share information over a network connection to a smartphone or other network capable devices.

internet protocol – is the set of rules used to send or receive information from or to a location on a network, including information about the source, destination and route. Each electronic location (host) has a unique address (the **IP address**) used to define the source and the destination.

Intrusion Detection Systems (IDS) – a computer program that monitors and inspects electronic communications that pass through it, with the purpose to detect, log (record) and raise alerts on any suspected malicious or otherwise unwanted streams of information. This is a variation from an **intrusion detection and prevention system** as it has no ability to block the activity, only to monitor, inspect and alert.

Intrusion Detection and Prevention Systems (IDPS) – a computer program that monitors and inspects electronic communications that pass through it, with the purpose and ability (i) to block and log (record key information) about any known malicious or otherwise unwanted streams of information and (ii) to log and raise alerts about any other traffic that is suspected (but not confirmed) to be of a similar nature. These are usually placed in the communication path to allow the prevention (dropping or blocking of **packets**) to occur. They can also clean some electronic data to remove any unwanted or undesirable packet components.

Intrusion Prevention Systems (IPS) – see **intrusion detection and prevention systems**. A small variant on an IPS, compared to an IDPS is that it may not collect any detection information and may only serve to block (prevent) unwanted traffic based on direct rules or instructions it receives.

IOC – see **Indicators of Compromise**.

IoT – see **Internet of Things.**

IP address – see **internet protocol.**

IPS – see **Intrusion Prevention System.**

J is for Java

Java – a programming language designed primarily for internet programs.

jump drive – a portable electronic data storage device usually attachable through a **USB** port.

K is for Kill Chain

key – (in the context of cybersecurity) is a set of information that can be used to encode or decode encrypted information.

key management – the protection, storage, organizing and issue of **cryptographic** keys within an organization, sufficient to allow their **encryption** systems to be operated safely and effectively. Without the ability to correctly provide encryption keys to the right people and services at the right time, the ciphered information will either become inaccessible to the right people, or accessible to the wrong people.

key pair – see **asymmetric cryptography.**

keylogging – a form of malicious software that is used to record and disclose entries on a digital device. This type of malware is often used to collect credit card details, user identities and passwords.

kill chain – a conceptual cyber defense model that uses the structure of attack as a model to build a cyber defense strategy. The stages in an **advanced persistent threat** are typically used as a framework, with **cyber defense strategies** (detect, deny, disrupt, degrade, deceive, contain) considered at each stage. The model works on the basis that the earlier in the lifecycle that an attack can be detected and defeated, the lower the cost incurred and damage will be. The model can be a useful adjunct to defense strategy but also has inherent gaps, for example, it works best for internal organization networks but is less effective when applied to information outside of a defended perimeter. This model does very successfully emphasize that cyber attacks are much lower cost to deal with, when they are identified earlier in the **cyber attack lifecycle**.

kleptography – the study of **asymmetric backdoors** and other mechanisms that cyber attackers use to steal or hide information or access.

L is for Logic Bomb

least privilege – a basic security access practice of granting each person or user account with the minimum amount of **access rights** required to perform their role.

least significant bits – the part of a binary message furthest to the right (for example 100100**1**), sometimes used as a method to conceal information as an approach in **steganography** (the concealing of hidden messages).

logic bomb – a type of malicious software (malware) that only starts to operate when specific conditions are met. For example, if a particular date is reached or if a companion piece of malware is no longer detectable.

log management – the method of managing the significant volumes of computer generated files, such as event logs and audit trails, so that they are appropriately captured, collated, analyzed and archived.

M is for Malware

MAC address – abbreviation for **media access control address**. This is a unique identifier assigned to every single digital device with a network interface controller. If a device has multiple controllers, it may have multiple (unique) addresses, one for each controller. If the identifier (MAC address) is assigned by the manufacturer, part of it will include the manufacturer's identification number. There are several format conventions in existence. The identifier is used in network (including internet) communications.

MAC spoofing – impersonating the unique identifier (**MAC address**) of another network interface controller.

machine learning – the ability for a software program to review sets of information and extrapolate new theories or patterns that were not pre-programmed. This is essentially an advanced form of pattern recognition fused with an early type of **artificial intelligence**. The ability for programs to review and understand much larger sets of electronic information than humans, together with their ability to identify new trends and patterns, then propose new findings or opportunities. This is proving sometimes beneficial and sometimes controversial. One of the early issues is that the machine learning can reflect the bias or quality of the data, or lack the ethics of a human review. For example, an undisclosed fraud review machine learning program proposed profiling each claimant's country of origin as an indicator of the likelihood of fraud. As with regular forms of statistical analysis, care has to be taken with how information is understood to correlate; if a key data point is missing, the wrong conclusion will be drawn. As a simple example - Do I live in a certain country because I am overweight, am I overweight because I live in a certain country, or what other undisclosed factors may be involved?

macro virus – a form of malicious software designed to operate from within files used by other (usually legitimately installed) programs. For example, a word processing or spreadsheet file can contain sets of malicious instructions, if opened these instructions will be run by the word processing or spreadsheet software. This bypasses the opportunity for **anti-malware** to detect any new software installation, as the macro virus is leveraging and subverting an application that is already in place.

malware – shortened version of **mal**icious soft**ware**. A term used to describe the insertion of disruptive, subversive or hostile programs onto a digital device. These types of programs can be intentional or unintentional. Intentional versions are usually disguised or embedded in a file that looks harmless so they can intentionally compromise a device. There are many types of malware; **adware**, **botnets**, **computer viruses**, **ransomware**, **scareware**, **spyware**, **trojans** and **worms**, these are all examples of intentional malware. Unintentional malware can still disrupt a device or leak information; however, this can be through unintended poor build quality, bad design or insecure configuration. **Hackers** often use malware to mount cybersecurity attacks.

man-in-the-browser – a form of **malware** attack that modifies transactions within the web browser of the machine it is hosted on, so that covert additional transactions or transaction content can be modified without the users' knowledge or consent.

man-in-the-middle – the interception and relay by a third party of selected content between two legitimate parties, for the purpose of hijacking or adjusting an electronic transaction. For example, party 1 believes they have connected to their banking home page but is actually on an emulated screen offered by the intercepting attacker. As the log-in information is provided, the attacker can set-up a separate connection to the bank (party 2) and is able to respond to any challenge made by the bank by passing the same challenge back to the user (party 1). Once authorized in the transaction system, the attacker can now make transactions that have not been sanctioned by the user, without their immediate knowledge.

man-in-the-mobile – a form of **malware** for mobile phones that steals information and credentials.

master boot record – the first sector on any electronic device that defines what operating system should be loaded when it is initialized or re-started.

md5 hash – is a very clever algorithm that can be run against any block of data (electronic information) to produce a unique 32 character hexadecimal (numbers and letters) identifier. If even a single character or item of data in the block is changed – the hexadecimal identifier changes significantly. Only fully identical data blocks can ever create the same 32 character hexadecimal code. This allows for a wide range of security usages, for example, very large volumes of information (such as a forensically examined copy of a hard disk) can be compared to the original capture of the disk image and be shown to be completely as it was, without the need to do anything more than verify that the 32 digit hexadecimal value is the same as it was.

MDM – see **mobile device management.**

mega-breach – when the result of a **cyber attack** involves such a high level of catastrophic theft and/or such extensive intrusion that it leads to world press exposure. As the frequency and scale of breaches has increased, the threshold for newsworthy events has also increased.

memory – see **in-memory.**

metamorphic malware – a more sophisticated form of malware that changes all key parts of its code on each installation. **Polymorphic malware** uses less transformation techniques than this type of (metamorphic) malware as polymorphic malware usually only changes some key parts of its profile but retains the same core virus. See also **blended threat**.

metaverse – the utilization of technologies such as augmented or virtual reality to create environments more appealing and exciting to exist in than full reality, because they contain artificial components. The human impact of the metaverse is viewed as one of the most significant challenges and changes for mankind over the next 20 years. As an example, the likelihood is that people will have a higher propensity to form what they may consider to be more satisfying and less demanding personal relationships with synthetic constructions rather than other real people.

method – see **attack method.**

Mobile Device Management (MDM) – a technology used for the security administration of mobile devices such as tablets and smart phones. Able (for example) to remotely wipe information from a mobile device and control what applications and functions are permitted to be installed or run.

moving target defense – the use of frequent changes to multiple dimensions of a digital landscapes parameters and settings, to help decrease the potential for successful attack.

Moore's Law – created in 1965 by Gordon E. Moore. It states that over the history of computing, the processing power doubles approximately every two years.

multi-factor authentication – using more than one form of proof to confirm the identity of a person or device attempting to request access. There are usually three different categories of authentication types, (i) something you know [often a password] (ii) something you have [perhaps a security token or access card] and (iii) something you are [use of biometrics, for example fingerprint or facial recognition]. As an example, effective two-factor authentication would require that when access is being requested, proof would be required from at least two different categories.

N is for Network Segmentation

nagware – a form of software that persistently reminds the user that they should do something even though they might not want to. This is not usually considered malicious software but it does exhibit some unwanted features, disrupting the flow of the users' interaction with their device. Nagware is often used as partial payment for some forms of software, especially free software.

nanotechnology – incredibly small products and devices manufactured through the manipulation of items as small as atoms and molecules.

NAS – Network attached storage. A digital repository attached to a network where information can be stored.

NAT – acronym for **N**etwork **A**ddress **T**ranslation. This is a router protocol, typically used in firewalls and other devices to change (translate) the **IP address** between network addresses inside and outside a network gateway.

National Institute for Cybersecurity Education (NICE) – a US government initiative to help enhance the training and resources for the defense of digital technologies and the electronic information they contain and transact.

networks – the group name for a collection of devices, wiring and applications used to connect, carry, broadcast, monitor or safeguard data. Networks can be physical (use material assets such as wiring) or virtual (use applications to create associations and connections between devices or applications.) Usually the devices on a network will have some form of trusted permissions that allow them to pass and share packets of electronic information.

Network-based Intrusion Prevention Systems (NIPS) – see **Intrusion Prevention Systems**.

network forensics – a part of the **digital forensics** discipline, focused on being able to investigate and uncover evidence. This includes rebuilding and recovering electronic information from the devices used to connect and carry information between **endpoints**. Advances in defensive technology can now allow (for example) for all communicated data packages to be captured for a period of time. Where this technology is in place, even if the sending and receiving endpoint devices are initially unknown, information about what took place can still be acquired because the incoming and outgoing data packages that were communicated can be replayed in full. See also **indicators of compromise**.

network recording – a form of **cyber defense** that allows an organization to store a copy of all inbound and outbound data transmissions for a period of time. After any cyber incident, this allows the **incident response** team to review what data may have been compromised and also apply **digital forensics** to help identify the perpetrators.

network segmentation – splitting a single collection of devices, wiring and applications that connect, carry broadcast, monitor or safeguard data, into smaller sections. This allows for more discrete management of each section, allowing greater security to be applied in sections of the highest value and also enabling smaller sections to be impacted in the event of a malware infection or other disruptive event.

network sniffer – see **sniffing.**

network traffic analysis – the act of recording, reviewing and inspecting key information about the **data** that is transacted over **digital devices** and infrastructure used to connect and transport electronic information. This technique is used extensively by **intrusion detection and prevention systems** and other network security sensors. The information collected can also be used towards **advanced threat detection** and **digital forensics** as an **indicator of compromise**.

NFC – acronym for **N**ear **F**ield **C**ommunication. A method of extremely short range data communication that uses electromagnetic induction and usually operates by touching NFC enabled devices together or from a maximum range of up to 2 inches or 5 cm.

NICE – see **National Institute for Cybersecurity Education.**

non-repudiation – the act of ensuring that a users electronic activity has sufficient identity checks and audit evidence in place so that it cannot be refuted or denied by the person performing the action.

O is for OWASP

open source – an **application**, other computer program or software building block where the software code is made publicly available for expansion, use or modification by anybody.

This makes it very cheap to use but also opens up higher potential for malicious subversion, especially if subverted versions of the work are incorporated into systems that are intended to be secure.

openSSL – an **open source** version of the Secure Sockets Layer protocol used to help provide **authentication** and **cryptographic** security between two parties. This protocol is used widely on internet web servers and web sites to help prevent interception, intrusion and falsification as communications are passed between a legitimate host and the intended recipient of the data.

Open Web Application Security Project – see **OWASP.**

OWASP – the **O**pen **W**eb **A**pplication **S**ecurity **P**roject is an online community that aims to create free, public resources to help improve the security of software. For example, they maintain lists of the leading vulnerabilities and security controls.

P is for Patch Management

PaaS – acronym meaning **P**latform **a**s **a S**ervice. Applications are developed and deployed on platforms. This type of **cloud** service allows the development and deployment of new applications to take place for a lower cost and with faster scalability than setting up the equivalent in a private network. The cost benefits and scalability are achieved through the use of shared infrastructure and pre-configured virtual machines. Where the platform is public (open to the internet) and needs to be secure, additional security is required, when compared to a private platform, to achieve the equivalent perimeter protection. See also **cloud**.

packet – (in the context of electronic communication) is a bundle of electronic information grouped together for transmission. The bundle usually includes **control information** to indicate the destination, source and type of content, and the content (user information) itself.

packet-filtering – passing or blocking bundles of electronic information inbound or outbound based on rules. For example, if a known threat uses a particular size, format and type of data package (packet), then a rule can be put in place, on either an advanced firewall or similar device, to block content that matches those parameters from leaving or entering a network. See also **packet**. Also known as **content filtering**.

packet sniffer – see **sniffing**.

password – a secret string of characters (letters, numbers and other special characters) that can be used to gain entry to a **digital device**, **application** or other service.

password salting – see **salting**.

patch management – a controlled process used to deploy critical, interim updates to software on digital devices. The release of a software 'patch' is usually in response to a critical flaw or gap that has been identified. Any failure to apply new interim software updates promptly can leave open security **vulnerabilities** in place. As a consequence, promptly applying these updates (**patch management**) is considered a critical component to maintaining effective cybersecurity.

payload – the part of the data in a transmission that is the usable content rather than the packaging (the cargo). In the context of cybersecurity, this term is often used to refer to the harmful data (malware for example) that is attempted to be pushed into a target digital device, network or system. For example, an attacker **exploits** a **vulnerability** to deliver their **payload** of **malware**.

payload analysis – the recording, review and study of the primary data content (electronic information) contained in network transmission **packets**. This can be used to detect any unexpected, unauthorized or unwelcome incoming or outgoing information transactions, for example, – to help detect or prevent **malware** from entering a network, or to help detect or prevent confidential information from leaving a network. This can also be used as an **indicator of compromise**.

penetration – (in the context of cybersecurity) intrusion.

penetration test (also known as an **attack and penetration test** or **pen. test**) – checks and scans on any application, system or website to identify any potential security gaps (**vulnerabilities**) that could be exploited. Usually these checks emulate the same techniques that could be used by an attacker and are performed in a test area. This is to prevent any inadvertent operational disruption. The checks are typically conducted before any application or site is first used and also on a periodic (repeating) basis, for example, each time the program is updated or every 6 months. Any significant gaps must be addressed (fixed) in a timeframe appropriate to the scale of the risk. See also **pivoting**.

penetration tester – a person that performs simulated attempts at attack on a target system or application on behalf of the organization that owns or controls it. See also **penetration test** and **pivoting**.

periscope up – when people hold a smart device up at head height or higher to capture an event on the device camera.

personally identifiable information (PII) – any combination of information that can directly or indirectly distinguish (identify) who a specific individual is.

persistence – to seek continued existence despite opposition.

persistent (non-reflective) cross-site scripting – a more devastating form of web vulnerability that can impact large numbers of users due to security gaps in the design of some web applications. Unwanted and unexpected code (programs) can be pushed to an application server by an attacker. When a legitimate user accesses the compromised web application, the attackers' script (mini program or link) can then be run automatically without any further user action. This is generally considered a critical risk category because it can target all users of an application. See also **reflective (non-persistent) cross site scripting**.

phantom vibration – when you think you felt your smart device vibrate but find out that it did not, or realize that there is no smart device in that area of your body right now.

phishing – using an electronic communication (for example email or instant messaging) that pretends to come from a legitimate source, in an attempt to get sensitive information (for example a password or credit card number) from the recipient or install malware to their device. The methods of phishing have evolved so that the message can simply contain a link to an internet location where **malware** is situated or include an attachment (such as a PDF or Word document) that installs **malware** when opened. The malware can then be used to run any number of unauthorized functions, including stealing information from the device, replicating further malware to other accessible locations, sharing the user screen and logging keyboard entries made by the user. Less complex forms of phishing can encourage the recipient to visit a fake but convincing version of a website and disclose password or other details.

physical security – measures designed to deter, prevent, detect or alert unauthorized real world access to a site or material item.

PII – see **personally identifiable information.**

pivoting – a method used by **penetration testers** and attackers to leverage a point of infiltration as a route for easier access to compromise, infect and/or attack further systems and networks.

PKI – see **public key infrastructure.**

policy – (i) a high level statement of intent, often a short document, providing guidance on the principles an organization follows. For example, a basic security policy document could describe the intention for an enterprise to ensure all locations (physical and electronic) where information they are accountable for, must remain secure from any unauthorized access. A policy does not usually describe the explicit mechanisms or specific instruction that would be used to achieve or enforce the intentions it expresses; this would be described in the **procedure.** (ii) Alternatively, it can also be used to mean the settings (including security settings) inside a software program or operating system.

polymorphic malware – malicious software that can change its attributes to help avoid detection by anti-malware. This mutation process can be automated so that the function of the software continues but the method of operation, location and other attributes may change. See also **metamorphic malware** and **blended threat**.

port – part of the techniques that help organize the diverse range of communications and services that can take place between electronic devices and computer programs. By assigning a specific value (a **port number**) when sending information, the receiver can know what type of information it should be and how to process it. This information can also be used by security devices such as **firewalls** to help allow or deny certain communication types.

port number – used as part of an electronic communication to denote the method of communication being used. This allows the **packet** to be directed to a program that will know what to do with it.

preventive control – (see also **control**) a method of security defense used to stop issues before they can become problematic. For example, **multi-factor authentication** assists in stopping unauthorized access from ever occurring and is therefore considered a preventive control.

private key – a unique encryption device or formula provided to a specific individual or specific service as one part on an encryption system. See **asymmetric cryptography**.

privileged account – an electronic user access right that has elevated permissions to allow it to perform system, application, database or other digital landscape management functions. Usually, this form of access requires additional controls and supervision to ensure the elevated privileges are fully accountable and are not misused. Most forms of **cyber attack** seek to gain this form of access as these types of accounts have control over their **digital landscape**.

privileged account management – the systems, technologies and processes used to monitor and control the activities of **privileged accounts.**

procedure – provides guidance or specific instruction on the process (method) that should be used to achieve an objective. Traditionally provided as a document available to appropriate personnel but increasingly replaced by enforcing steps in computer systems. In a traditional quality model, procedures may reside under a **policy** as an explicit instruction for how a particular objective of a policy is met. See also **policy** definition (i).

protocol – (in the context of electronic communication) is a set of established rules used to send information between different electronic locations. They provide a standard that can be used to send or receive information in an expected and understandable format, including information about the source, destination and route. Examples of protocols include, **internet protocol (IP)**, **hyper text transfer protocol (HTTP)**, **file transfer protocol (FTP)**, **transmission control protocol (TCP)**, **border gateway protocol (BGP)** and **dynamic host configuration protocol (DHCP)**.

public – (in the context of cybersecurity) indicates that the artifact used in any prefix or suffix is openly available and accessible over the internet.

public key cryptography – see **asymmetric cryptography.**

public key encryption – see **asymmetric cryptography**.

Public key infrastructure – the set of hardware, applications and processes needed to manage public-key encryption

PUPs – acronym for **P**otentially **U**nwanted **P**rogram. Describes a type of software that the user may have consented to download but that performs some undesirable or potentially malicious functions. Often this kind of software may be bundled in with other software that the user has consented to download.

pwned – domination or humiliation of a rival, originating from video game play but also applied to cyber security attacks.

Q is for Quarantine

quarantine – the act of isolating any known or suspected malware so that it can do no further damage to digital information and assets, usually as a pre-cursor to removal or examination. See also **containment**.

R is for Risk

rainbow tables – a set of precomputed encryption values that can be used to reverse engineer items such as hash values back to their unencrypted value. These can be used to help crack (reveal) an encrypted value. As an example, most short hash values that use standard hash techniques can be entered into Google to reveal their unencrypted value.

ransomware – a form of malicious software (**malware**) that prevents or restricts usage of one or more digital devices or applications until a sum of money is paid. **Cryptoviral extortion** is an example of the techniques used to perform this type of attack.

RAT – a **r**emote **a**ccess **t**ool or **r**emote **a**ccess **t**rojan are used as forms or components of malware to help attackers gain control over a target computer or other digital device.

recovery point objective (RPO) – the maximum amount of data loss or corruption that can be permitted (often expressed as a time) in the event of a system disruption. This in turn sets the

backup and other failsafe requirements for a system. For example, a hotel or air-flight booking system may have a zero tolerance to any data loss (no transactions can be permitted to be lost – because they cannot be recovered through any other means) requiring that the system has an infallible method of logging all transactions, so they can always be recovered. Note: This is a different parameter from system availability as it only covers if (and how much) entered data can be lost to the owner. For availability – see **recovery time objective (RTO)**.

recovery time objective (RTO) – the targeted amount of days, hours, minutes or seconds that a service, application or process must be restored within, if it is subject to any disruption. This should be based on the **availability** rating set by the owner (the **recovery time objective** must not exceed the **availability** requirement).

red team – when testing for potential exploits on any critical or sensitive system, infrastructure or website, a team of penetration testers is usually used. This term is used to describe the group of penetration testers working together on this type of objective.

reflective (non-persistent) cross-site scripting – a form of web vulnerability that can impact individual users due to security gaps in the design of some web applications. Unwanted and unexpected code (programs) can be run on a user's machine if they can be persuaded to click or interact with content that may look legitimate, but is in fact a link to malware. This is generally considered a lower risk category because it can only target individual users (not the host application) and requires considerable effort for low return from hackers, plus additional user action. See also **persistent (non-reflective) cross site scripting**.

residual risk – refers to the remaining possibility of loss and impact after security **controls** (the risk response) for an item have been applied.

resilience – the ability to remain functional and capable in the face of threat or danger, or to return to function rapidly following any disruption.

risk – a situation involving exposure to significant impact or loss. In formal frameworks, risk can be quantified using probability (often expressed as a percentage) and impact (often expressed as a financial amount). Other parameters for risk can include proximity (how soon a potential risk may be encountered and information about what assets, services, products and processes could be affected).

risk assessment – a systematic process for the proactive detection of potential hazards or gaps on an existing or planned activity, asset, service, application, system or product.

risk-based – an approach that considers the financial impact of a failure, its probability and proximity to determine its' comparative significance and priority for treatment.

risk register – a central repository that contains entries for each potential, significant loss or damage exposure. Usually there is a minimum materiality threshold, for example a minimum potential financial loss value that must be met or exceeded before an entry in the repository is required. If a risk does occur, it technically becomes an issue (rather than a risk). Issues can continue to be tracked within a risk register until the impact has been successfully managed and the root cause/s have been resolved to the extent that the risk is not likely to repeat,

rogueware – see **scareware.**

rootkit – a set of software tools that can be used by **attackers** to gain privileged access and control to the core (root) of the target device, where commands can be more easily run. Part of the function of a rootkit usually includes hiding malicious files and processes to help avoid detection and removal of the malware.

router – a device used to define the path for data packets (electronic information) to follow when they flow between networks.

S is for Steganography

salting – is a security concealment process often applied to password storage security. When a user selects a password, it usually needs to be a relatively short string of characters and numbers and may not be unique (other users may have selected the same password). The password is usually concealed using a process known as **hashing**. Salting is the process of adding a long, unique and random string of characters to the password before it is subject to hashing. This is to ensure that (for example) if two users choose the same password, the hash value will still be different because the value represents the combination of the password and the unique random information. It also helps to reduce the possibility of being able to perform a reverse lookup of the 'hash' value to uncover the password through search engines and rainbow tables.

sandboxing – a method used by some anti-malware solutions to temporarily place content in a safe area (usually for a matter of seconds) to observe its behavior before allowing it into the real domain. This is used to help identify malware in addition to traditional **signature** techniques. Some advanced malware is now written to take account of this technique and have a time delay before exhibiting any rogue behavior, thereby circumventing this defensive technique.

scareware – malicious software that is designed to persuade people into buying an antidote, usually masquerading as a commercial malware removal tool or anti-virus package, but in reality provided by the attacker.

script bunny – see **script kiddies**.

script kiddies – an attacker with little to no coding (programming) or technical skills that makes use of available scripts, codes and packages to gain unauthorized access to **digital devices, applications, systems** and/or **networks**. Also known as **script bunnies** and **skiddies**.

secure configuration – ensuring that when settings are applied to any item (device or software), appropriate steps are always taken to ensure (i) **default accounts** are removed or disabled, (ii) shared accounts are not used and (iii) all protective and defensive control in the item use the strongest appropriate setting/s.

secure file transfer protocol (also known as **SFTP**) – see **file transfer protocol (FTP)**.

secure hyper text transfer protocol (SHTTP) – see **hyper text transfer protocol**.

security analytics – the collation of log file and record information from technologies and processes designed to detect and defend a *digital landscape*, for the purpose of reviewing and defining any significant patterns, trends or gaps in the security posture.

security architecture – a model designed to specify the features and controls across a **digital landscape** that help it to prevent, detect and control any attempts at disruption or unauthorized access. The model will also ensure that all data exchanges are subject to appropriate standards sufficient to ensure that the **data controller**s chain of custody commitments are maintained.

security event – a term used to describe a minor disruption to the digital landscape that is thought to be unintentional. Examples include a single failed device or a single user forgetting their password. Unusual patterns of security events can be an indicator of a security incident.

Security Incident & Event Management – see **SIEM**.

security incident – the intentional damage, theft and/or unauthorized access that has direct or indirect impact to any part of an organizations information, systems, devices, services or products.

security incident responder – a person who assists in the initial analysis and response to any known or suspected attempt at damage, interruption or unauthorized access to an organizations information systems or services.

SHA1 – acronym for Secure Hash Algorithm 1. This is a legacy **cryptographic** standard designed in around 1995 that is no longer considered secure. It was followed by SHA-2 in 2001 and SHA-3 in 2015. A challenge with all forms of **encryption** is that their security tends to be time based; encryption considered strong or undefeatable at one point in time becomes defeatable years later as computing power increases.

shellshock – is the name given to a family of security bugs, discovered in September 2014. These bugs can be used to **attack** certain devices that work on the Unix bash shell platform if they have not had appropriate up to date software **patch management** applied. Vulnerable (unpatched) systems can be compromised to allow the attacker to gain unauthorized access. It was initially assigned the **CVE identifier** of CVE-2014-6271 but after initial reporting, additional vulnerabilities were identified. Also known as **bashdoor**.

SIEM – abbreviation for **security incident and event**

management. This is a name given to the process and team that will manage any form of minor or major interruption to an enterprises digital landscape.

single point (of) accountability (SPA or **SPOA)** – the principle that all critical assets, processes and actions must have clear ownership and traceability to a single person. The rationale is that the absence of a defined, single owner is a frequent cause of process or asset protection failure. Shared ownership is regarded as a significant security gap due to the consistent demonstration of increased probability of flaws persisting where accountability across more than one person is present.

single point (of) failure – a vulnerability that is so significant, it can be used to create devastating disruption to an entire organization.

signatures – (in the context of cybersecurity) are the unique attributes, for example, file size, file extension, data usage patterns and method of operation, that identify a specific computer program. Traditional anti-malware and other security technologies can make use of this information to identify and manage some forms of rogue software or communications.

singularity (the) – the predicted point in time when artificial intelligence exceeds human intelligence.

skiddie – abbreviated form of **script kiddie**.

smishing – a **phishing** attack that uses the simple message service (SMS) to send a malicious link or file to a phone as a text message. If the malicious link or attachment is opened, the device may be compromised. This form of attack can also use the MMS (multi-media service).

sniffing – the act of monitoring and analyzing traffic to identify and resolve problems at a network (network sniffer), data packet

(packet sniffer) or other level (for example wireless sniffer).

social engineering – The act of constructing relationships, friendships or other human interactions for the purpose of getting the recipient to perform an action or reveal information. The action or information revealed has the hidden purpose to achieve a nefarious objective, such as acquiring intelligence about the security, location or vulnerability of assets or even gaining the persons trust to open an internet link or document that will result in a malware foothold being created.

software program – see **application**.

SPA – see **single point of accountability.**

spear phishing – a more targeted from of **phishing**. This term describes the use of an electronic communication (for example email or instant messaging) that targets a particular person or group of people (for example employees at a location) and pretends to come from a legitimate source. In this case, the source may also pretend to be someone known and trusted to the recipient, in an attempt to get sensitive information (for example a password or credit card number).

spoofing – concealing the true source of electronic information by impersonation or other means. Often used to bypass internet security filters by pretending the source is from a trusted location.

spyware – a form of malware that covertly gathers and transmits information from the device it is installed on.

SSID – acronym for **S**ervice **S**et **Id**entifier. This is the set of up to 32 characters that are used to recognize a particular Wireless Local Area Network (WLAN) connection on Wi-Fi routers and other access points. A list of the values can be seen when any device scans for visible wireless connections.

SSL – is an acronym for Secure Sockets Layer. This is a method (protocol) for providing encrypted communication between two points in a digital landscape. For example, this could be between a **web server** (the computer hosting a web service or web site) and a **web browser** (the program that the recipient uses to view the web page, for example, Internet Explorer). In the **URL** (the internet address visible to the user), the use of SSL is denoted by an 'https:' prefix.

stacked risk – the phenomena of allowing seemingly separate potential issues with potential impact (**risks**) affecting the same **digital landscape** to accumulate. Without adequate identification and resolution, individual risks can form a toxic accumulation of issues that can be leveraged together to create a risk substantially greater than their individual components suggest. **Mega-breaches** are usually the result of stacked risk in combination with a motivated attacker.

stateful protocol analysis detection – is a method used by **intrusion detection** systems to identify malicious or unwanted communications. This method analyses **packets** to determine if the source, destination, size and routing (**protocol**) is significantly different from its usual format.

static source code testing – see **static testing.**

static testing – (in the context of cybersecurity) to assess the security standards and potential **vulnerabilities** within the source code (program) of an **application**. This is a form of **white-box** testing. See also **dynamic testing**.

statistical anomaly based detection – is a method used by some **intrusion detection systems** to identify malicious or unwanted communications. The program reviews the metrics it collects to identify any groups of communication behaviors that are unusual or anomalous.

steganalysis – the study of messages, image files and other objects to determine if and how they are carrying any concealed information. See also **steganography**.

steganography – to create or write concealed information of one type inside another message, image, file or other object so that only the sender and recipient know it is present. This is different from **encryption** because the information can still be in plain text; it is only the pattern or distribution used to conceal the information that may hide its presence. Derived from the Greek for 'concealed writing'. This technique is used extensively in cyber attacks to move unwanted and otherwise unauthorized information in and out of secure locations, by disguising instructions and stolen data packages as standard communications. Steganography is often combined with encryption to make the covert communications even more difficult to identify and defend against. See also **image steganography**.

structured query language injection (SQL injection) – a form of security exploit that takes advantage of security design flaws in web forms. Within some web pages, there are forms that users can complete. If a web form does not sufficiently validate (check) the content of information returned to it, an attacker can create longer entries than expected that include commands that allow unauthorized and unexpected values into the database. The consequences can be the corruption of the database and transactions.

stuxnet – a family of malware designed to target **controls systems**, originally believed to have been designed to disrupt the Iranian nuclear program. This malware includes a **worm** and a **rootkit**. It has typically been delivered to target environments through the use of an infected **usb** stick (**jump drive**). There are multiple **CVE identifiers** associated with this threat.

sucker list – an identified set of soft targets that are easy to take advantage of due to their propensity to pay **ransomware** demands and/or to have a weak security position.

symmetrical encryption – a method of changing plain text to and from secret (encoded) information using identical keys. In other words, the same key that is used to code the information into a secret format can be used to return the information to plain text. The **Advanced Encryption Standard (AES)** is an example of symmetrical encryption. See also **asymmetrical encryption.**

system administration – the configuration, maintenance and management functions in a digital landscape. This term can be applied to any digital device, electronic hardware, system, network, electronic service or application. This function requires the use of **privileged accounts**.

systems – groups of applications that operate together to serve a more complex purpose.

T is for Takedown

takedown – (i) the process of a defending organization rendering malware ineffective by removing its ability to perform its functions, for example, through **decapitation**. (ii) the process of an attacker making unavailable some or all of an organizations key systems or capabilities. (iii) to stop something working.

technical control – the use of an electronic or digital method to influence or command how it is, or is not, able to be used.

Technical Disaster Recovery Plan – an operational document that describes the exact process, people, information and assets required to put any electronic or digital system back in place within a timeline defined by the **business continuity plan**. If there are multiple **business continuity plans** that reference the same **technical disaster recovery plan**, the restoration time used must meet the shortest time specified in any of the documents.

threat – any source of potential harm to the digital landscape.

threat actors – an umbrella term to describe the collection of people and organizations that work to create **cyber attacks**. Examples of threat actors can include **cyber criminals**, **hacktivists** and nation states.

threatscape – a term that amalgamates **threat** and land**scape**. An umbrella term to describe the overall, expected methods (vectors) and types of cyber attackers, that an organization or individual might expect to be attacked through or by.

three lines of defense – (UK: **three lines of defence**) – a security assurance model from the (now replaced) UK Financial Services Authority (FSA). The first tier is the business (or operations level) who must own and be responsible for their information, systems and following due process. The second tier is the security management functions who provide the processes, controls, expertise and other framework items to allow the business to operate within acceptable security risk tolerances. The final tier is auditing those who verify that the first two tiers (lines of defense) are operating as they should.

transmission control protocol (TCP) – the standard method used for networks and the internet to send and receive data error free and in the same order as was originally intended.

transport layer security (TLS) – is a **cryptographic** protocol (set of rules) for allowing secure communication between two digital locations. It is the successor to the Secure Socket Layer protocol but is often referred to as being an **SSL** protocol. It is a form of **symmetrical encryption**.

triple DES – see **Data Encryption Standard**.

trojan – an application (software program) that appears to be harmless but actually conducts other unseen malicious and unauthorized activities.

trusted network – an area of interconnected **digital devices** where the security controls and assignment of authorizations and privileges are subject to a known and acceptable level of control. The opposite of an **untrusted network**,

two-factor authentication – see **multi factor authentication.**

U is for URL

unauthorized access – to gain entry without permission.

Unified Threat Management (UTM) – a security device that integrates a large number of security technologies and services. For example, a single gateway device that includes proxy firewall, intrusion prevention, gateway anti-malware and VPN functions.

untrusted network – an area of interconnected **digital devices** where the security controls and/or assignment of authorizations and privileges are not subject to any central or acceptable level of control.

URL – acronym for **u**niform **r**esource locator. This is essentially the address (or path) where a particular destination can be found. For example, the main address for the Google website is the URL http://www.google.com

US CERT – acronym for the **U**nited **S**tates **C**omputer **E**mergency **R**eadiness **T**eam.

USB – acronym for **U**niversal **S**erial **B**us. This is a standard connector that exists on most computers, smartphones, tablets and other physical electronic devices that allow other electronic devices to be connected. Used for attaching a range of devices including keyboards, mice, external displays, printers and external storage.

user behavior analysis – to collate and review information about how the people who are using a specific **digital landscape** perform their activities. This helps determine potential patterns and trends that can be used to design improved cyber defense and prevention measures.

user identity correlation – the collation and analysis of the access rights used by people within a specific authorization group to understand their patterns and behaviors for the purpose of validating their activities and detecting then preventing unexpected, undesirable or unauthorized access usage. For example, user access geo-location can identify and block a user identity if it is used from two very distributed locations in an impossibly short period of time.

ungenious – something that was intended to achieve one goal but has a spectacularly negative outcome instead.

V is for Vector

vector – another word for 'method', as in 'They used multiple vectors for the attack'

virtual private network (VPN) – a method of providing a secure connection between two points over a public (or unsecure) infrastructure, for example, to set-up a secure link between a remote company laptop in a hotel and the main company network.

virtual reality – a fully artificial, computer generated simulation of a real environment. See also **augmented reality.**

virus – a form of **malware** that spreads by infecting (attaching itself to) other files and usually seeks opportunities to continue that pattern. Viruses are now less common than other forms of malware. Viruses were the main type of malware in very early computing. For that reason, people often refer to something as a virus when it is technically another form of malware.

vishing – abbreviation for **voice ph**i**shing**. The use of a phone call or similar communication method (such as instant messaging) where the caller attempts to deceive the recipient in to performing an action (such as visiting a URL), or revealing information that can then be used to obtain unauthorized access to systems or accounts. Usually the ultimate purpose is to steal (or hold ransom) something of value. These types of calls are becoming extremely regular, as the criminal gangs involved may have stolen part of the recipients data already (name, phone number, …) to help persuade the person receiving the call that it is authentic. As a rule, if you did not initiate a call or message, you should never comply with any demand, especially to visit any webpage or link.

vulnerability – (in the context of cybersecurity) a weakness, usually in design, implementation or operation of software (including operating systems), that could be compromised and result in damage or harm.

W is for White Hat

web browser – the program a person uses on their device to view a web page. Examples of web browser programs include Internet Explorer and Firefox.

web server – is a computer that is used to host (provide) a web service or web site.

wet wiring – creating connections between the human nervous system and digital devices.

white-box testing (also known as **clear box testing**) – is the term used to describe a situation where the technical layout (or source code) of the computer program being tested has been made available for the security test. This makes the test easier and cheaper to perform but usually results in the identification of more issues than **black-box penetration testing**. White box testing can start early in the software lifecycle before an **application** has ever been installed in any production environments, making security fixes substantially cheaper and easier to apply.

white-hat – a security specialist who breaks into systems or networks by invitation (and with the permission) of the owner, with the intent to help identify and address security gaps.

white-listing – the restriction of 'allowed' internet sites or data packages to an explicit list of verified sources. For example, an organization operating a white-listing firewall can decide to only permit their network users to navigate to a restricted and verified list of internet websites. This is the opposite of **black-listing**.

white team – the people that act as referees during any **ethical hacking** exercise conducted between a **red team** and a **blue team**.

Wireless Intrusion Prevention Systems (WIPS) – a device that can be attached to a network and check the radio spectrum for rogue or other unauthorized access points, then take countermeasures to help close the threat down.

worm – a form of malicious software (malware) that seeks to find other locations that it can replicate to. This assists to both protect the malware from removal and increase the area of the **attack surface** that is compromised.

X is for XSS

XSS – see **cross-site scripting.**

XSS hole – see **cross-site scripting.**

Y is for Y2K

Y2K – acronym representing the year 2000 technology bug. Organizations spent hundreds of millions before the year 2000 ensuring their technologies were not taken out through the change of year in systems that had never been designed to cope with a 4 digit year change. Before the year 2000, there was a very real fear that major catastrophes could follow the date change (technology meltdown). As the year change came and went with little to no impact, many organizations felt they had been conned into excessive protective investments. Much of the resilience to adequate investments in cybersecurity can be attributed to the perceived over investment in resolving this technical item.

Z is for Zero Day

zbot trojan – see **Zeus.**

zero-day – refers to the very first time a new type of **exploit** or new piece of **malware** is discovered. At that point in time, none of the anti-virus, anti-malware or other defenses may be set-up to defend against the new form of exploit.

Zeus – is a **trojan** form of malware that can be used to target and steal confidential information (such as banking information) or install ransomware. It has been around for some time (since 2007) but is subject to repeated improvements and variations. It continues to be one of the main forms of malware used in many **drive-by downloads** and **phishing** attacks. Once in place, it can operate by **keylogging**, **man in the middle** attacks and other mechanisms.

zombie army – see **botnet.**

Numbers

0 day –see **zero-day** (exploit).

2FA – acronym for two factor authentication. See **multi-factor authentication.**

3DES – see **Triple DES**.

3 lines of defense – see **three lines of defense.**

ABOUT THE BOOK AND AUTHOR

If you ever watched the British sitcom Blackadder II, specifically the episode on creating the first English dictionary – writing this book has been very much like that. New words are emerging all the time as the subject evolves.

If you have any new words you would like included in the next edition, please feel free to tweet the author (@grcarchitect) with the suggested word and any definition you are willing for the book to freely use as a start point. The book avoided adding the 350 or so words that simply start with the word 'cyber'! The objective is to only include the most useful terms - and maybe some of the funnier ones.

Raef Meeuwisse is an active member of the ISACA London chapter. He compiled and re-wrote the synchronized security and privacy control framework for two, multi-billion dollar companies. His experience also includes managing a global vendor technology audit service, designing a fully integrated GRC platform, running massive global security programs, operating as a CISO and writing publications on cybersecurity. He enjoys speaking at very large conferences and at universities.

CPSIA information can be obtained
at www.ICGtesting.com
Printed in the USA
LVOW04s1959211016

509751LV00008B/457/P